KNOW WHEN TO RIDE

DEVRET CLARKE

DEVRET CLARKE

KNOW WHEN TO RIDE

WRITTEN
BY:

DEVRET CLARKE

Copyright © 2022 Devret Clarke

ISBN: 9798425166456
Imprint: Independently published

~ *Peace and Blessings* ~

I thank you for the purchase of my 26th book, (24th published), "KNOW WHEN TO DIDE". This is all about being true, being loyal, being smart, and always being true to self (morals and values).

As you read on, start to question your own life, and decision which make you who you are, as well as your surroundings.

I thank you for riding with me along the way of my journey, for those who have been purchasing my books, and reading, learning, and sharing. I hope I made this ride worth your time, as I put my best efforts into this, and hope that is helps you along your journey.

Know when to ride.

— Devret Clarke -
website: devretclarke.ca

CHAPTERS

CHAPTER ONE

ARE YOU A RIDER

?

"Are you a rider?
Will you be there when I have nothing?
For if you do, I will remember you
when I have something.

Loyalty is hard to come by.
For me,
the most loyal,
has to be the Most High.

He's been there,
through the stormy rain
through all seasons
HE remained the same.

Taught me to be a man,
so that I can stand on my own two.
Been a rider for me,
and I'm a rider for HIM too."

When I talk about a rider, I talk about someone that is going to be up with you at all times. I say, "up", because that is where you should be, as many are used to saying, "are you down with me?". That sounds negative. It's all about the rise, and the come up, so are are you up with me? Are you a rider? A rider is someone that is going to be with you through thick and thin. That someone that happens to be with you when the storm hits, as well as when the storm passes by, and sunshine is shinning. Not all of us have riders. Most riders will not care for what happens along the way. Just as long as they prove their loyalty. When it's time to ride, they are going to be on call, ready, and on stand by, or willing to drop whatever they are doing to support you.

When you have a true friend, a brother, a sister, someone that will be there for you at all times when needed the most, it is important to appreciate that/those individual(s), and treat them the same. For not many are out there that are loyal from the soil. From the ground up. I know riders. Most are from childhood, and that is where it stopped. Not due to any other reason, but due to the fact of moving away from one another. There was a family with a close friend that was a rider for our family, at all times. Never took advantage of us, nor stole from us, and was never one to go against the grain. Many times he would be there to fight with us, and be up with us in friendship, no matter the circumstance, whether it be of low financial state, or well off. With, or without, he was always there. As we grew older, we moved apart, however, it's all love when we see one another. I remember being at a bus stop, and seeing this brother in a crowded bus that I didn't take for the same reason of being overly crowded, but he was in there hailing me up, making sure he shouted me out, even though I didn't see him, yet he seen me, and then I caught his attention, by hitting the bus window, so that I could see him. As he was there, he saw me, and could have easily remained silent, due to being on that crowded bus, but instead, he made sure to grab my attention, and stuff like that keeps me honouring the bond that we once had, for he is a solid dude for that. And likewise, we always remember to bring up his name in conversation, in a good way, knowing he is a loyal person, sincere brother, from the time we knew him. Although I do not like putting names in my books, as seasons change, I will shout out to him now, and say, "peace to my brother from a different mother, and father, Shane Alexander", hope all is well with you and yours. Much respect always. A true rider. There were a few more riders, but from the soil, no one tops that brother.

Others along the way, showed that they were not so loyal. I remember having close friends from two years old until grade school. Once High School hit, they changed up, and showed me their true character. One two occasions, I can recall two close individuals who I considered best friends at the ages of 2-10. One, made sure to tell me, once he goes to high school, he will not be cool with me, knowing he will then ride with his brothers friends. Hearing that, only showed how fake everything was, and how reality started to kick in. For I was still young, and immature, yet we were all the same, until we grew up. Nonetheless, I seen him from time to time, and we greeted one another, but that's where it stopped. I never went against the grain, nor owed him loyalty, yet I was the man that kept true to all, until that seal is broken.

Another time, when we started getting older, and this next "friend" who came later, roughly two years left within grade school, and we ended up going to the same middle school. This dude showed me his disloyalty, and did similar to the last one, who pretended like he didn't know me, nor wanted to be seen around me. Seeing his behaviour, made me look at him as a sellout. For we never fell out before, but for him to end up finding out he was in the same class, wanted to change classes, and eventually changed school, without even coming to me like a brother, and saying "how come". Yet, it was cool to know that he was fake, and I stayed true. It doesn't matter the circumstances we were at, it came down to the fact, this guy only forgot how I took him under my arms when he came to our school back then. I pretty much made sure to make it comfortable for him to be there, and allow the group of friends that I had, to know he was cool, and up with us, as he lived close to my block, and I was cool with his cousin. Since then, I seen him from time to time, and he always says "what's up", however, it is not sincere. Knowing his cousin and I had no beef, for I spoke to him during high school, and it was always respect. Funny thing is, he would ways tell people around him later on, how I was him best friend during grade school, and all. But that meant nothing, for that diss that he had done, made me look at him different, and in truth, I am thankful, I am not like any of these guys, for I am me, and needed to go down this journey alone, which made me the man that I am today. I'm a grown man today, so I do not have no malice nor hate towards any of them. It just suck to know that the foundation of friendship, is usually formed at that age. Grow together, and ride together, however, I have no regrets riding alone. For the true friend was in me.

Don't get the term "rider" mixed up with "kiss-ass" as that is not the same thing. For many kiss-ass people will "ride" with you just because they are on your sack. They will be with you at all times, just to gas you up, and/or because they have nothing better to do with their time. Nobody needs a kiss-ass around, unless you lack self-respect, and need someone to gas you up along the way. If you need that, you may as well build your house upon sand, where the foundation will not stand.

Matthew 7:24-27
<u>King James Version</u>

24 Therefore whosoever heareth these sayings of mine, and doeth them, I will liken him unto a wise man, which built his house upon a rock:

25 And the rain descended, and the floods came, and the winds blew, and beat upon that house; and it fell not: for it was founded upon a rock.

26 And every one that heareth these sayings of mine, and doeth them not, shall be likened unto a foolish man, which built his house upon the sand:

27 And the rain descended, and the floods came, and the winds blew, and beat upon that house; and it fell: and great was the fall of it.

Be careful of the "occasional rider", for they only ride when it is convenient for themselves to benefit. They will not ride when it is time for important thing to go about, when it comes to your business. They shy away when you need them the most. When it's time for you to go about your business that is soothing to their ears, they will yell "shotgun", as in front seat right next to you. That is when you need to know when to push away those who are not sincere.

Real riders will tell you the truth, such as a brother, a true sister, and even a friend. You need people around you that will tell you the truth, and protect you at all times. They have good intentions for your life, and care for you. The truth is important, for it can help your existence, and hearing that truth from a friend, is important. If I'm doing wrong, be there, to teach me to do right. Correct me, not kiss my ass, because you are comfortable, afraid, or not caring from my well best. Many times in life, we all need that person who we trust, to be that rider, and tell us exactly how it is, and be bold in the process. For the criticism coming from that individual will not be as harmful, knowing the relationship, compared to an outsider who will take advantage.

As you see within the cover art picture, a car in

the cover of this book, that doesn't mean being a rider, must always be in a car. It is a figure of speech that symbolizes, being loyal, honest, and true. Being a rider is not about gangster living. Though it may appear so, that is not my aim, nor my message. I am talking about the average person out here that is loyal to their family and friends, and in some cases within the relationship, but being loyal to self too. Being a rider is all about being there. Most importantly, for the believers, be a rider for the LORD. For HE will always be rider for you. To ask the question, "are you a rider?", if you know the qualities of the Most High, you should know the qualities within those surrounding you, who have the same/similar features.

Deuteronomy 7:9
<u>King James Version</u>

9 Know therefore that the LORD thy God, he is God, the faithful God, which keepeth covenant and mercy with them that love him and keep his commandments to a thousand generations;

CHAPTER
TWO

FAKE RIDERS
(A SET UP FOR DESTRUCTION)

"Fake riders,
never will I trust you.
Leave me feeling all the time in disgust too.
Your ways are crooked,
you are not sincere.
You're only around
because everyone real is here.
What you pretend to be,
I do not care
for when I look in your eyes
All I see is fear.
I know it's not fare,
a character that you're not,
but who taught you to be fake?
If I were to allow you in my circle
it's like having a garden,
with a well known snake.
An established foundation
with your intentions to break.
You can never be true,
because you're artificially fake"

Touching more on the topic of "kiss-asses", no one needs them around. Don't be a cling-on, kiss-ass, nor a follower without a cause. Just as much as you do not need these type of people in your life, you don't need to be that type of person yourself neither. Touching first on "kiss-asses and cling-on" type people. When you are so, expect to never be respected as a real one, which is someone who is not fake. It's see through by the real immediately. When you are a kiss-ass and cling-on, you are fake, and no one respects you, especially real ones, for real ones cannot stand anything fake. For real ones, know real from fake, and once you show how fake you are, don't expect to ever get that respect from a real one. Being a kiss-ass rider, only shows how much you are willing to go along with everything, and anything that the main individual is doing. This is a form of a broken trust that cannot be established. You agree at times, even when you know in your heart that you disagree with that being said, or done. Being a cling-on is similar for those who do so, are likewise going to agree with everything, but also won't leave when given the push, which is the sign to say "goodbye" today, and meet up again at a later date. A cling on reaches out often, even too often, like calling five minutes after you just spoke, just to be on the line with you. I've had that happen to me a couple of times, and unfortunately with other guys, trying to befriend me, while they would behave in a cling-on manner, by calling too often, and in most cases, to say nothing but the same things as before, "what are you doing?", ext. I had to cut those people off quickly, as again, if you are real, you only want real ones around you.

Now, let me touch on those who are followers without a cause. Never should you ride with another individual without a cause. A family member, or a very close friend is okay, however, when you are with someone else who you are just "okay" with, and riding along without a cause, it shows you are putting your life in danger, only to know that their journey is different from your own. You don't know what can come about and can happen, for without knowing, you are exposing yourself to anything possible. Not every situation is going to be a dangerous one, however, when you don't know, you just don't know. Strive not to be with busy-bodies, for you may just end up facing the same troubles heading that persons way.

Do not be in another persons life who you are not in the same path with, meaning along the same journey, for you may just be labelled as the same. For example, a cowards that gets his lunch money took, and you are walking with him, while witnessing him get his money taken away from him, and do nothing to support nor ride with your friend, to secure his money. While standing there, you will be looked upon as disloyal, and even a coward just as your friend who gets his lunch money taken away from him. So, strive not with that person.

Proverbs 3:30
<u>King James Version</u>

30 Strive not with a man without cause, if he have done thee no harm.

There are fake riders who are always going to pick the side of the majority. There was a time when I was in a little "beef" with someone who never addressed their problems to my face. Instead, he would go around spreading rumours, and lies about me to others, hoping they will take on his "beef", as they did. Though he is older, this clown was far from a man, for he was a coward. Now, this clown would beat on his wife, and even argue with her constantly, while bullying her often. All the people that this clown would spread rumours and lies about me to, they never questioned his actions towards his wife, even a couple times, giving her a black eye. This clown of a man, put hands on his wife, and shamed her by putting a mark of anger and abuse on her face, while he never came to me about a thing in a manly form, for I wish he would have. What would you call that kind of man? Not a coward? So, what would you call someone who knows this type of man's actions, and still supports him, while trying to get at me? Of course a fake rider. They choose to not address his situations, but attempted to address issues that he had with me, while not even facing me either, and they did the same shit as him, but worse, while doing childish things, and again, not to my face. These are fake riders, and are nothing but pussies. I remember hearing one of those clown supporters say, "I got your back", towards that same elderly man, as if he could do anything to me, even if I wanted to do something to his face. As he mentions, he has his back, who has his front? For I face my enemies face to face.

Jeremiah 1:8
<u>King James Version</u>

8 Be not afraid of their faces: for I am with thee to deliver thee, saith the LORD.

Those fake riders should have been real enough to check this clown to address the ignorance being done unto his wife first. And then even check him to question how come he can do such things unto his wife, but not unto me? That is why these losers supporting him, are considered fake riders. True riders need everything to be solid. The foundation is where everything starts. They will not be real with their own, but will pretend to be real against the false enemy. For if I were the real enemy, they would treat me like one, instead of dodging, and hiding while doing dirt. Fake riders are everywhere. For they are simple minded, and lack any form of realness to them.

They will avoid real situations at all times, while only pretending to be "down". They go where the wind blows, and only go where the majority of people are, for it is comforting to win a battle with more soldiers, and not needing to put much of a fight up. For this sake, they tend to only join the majority, in order to win the battle, and look tough, while posing in the background. It reminds me of people from school who only run their mouth when in groups of people, against one individual, only to appear bad-ass. They are fake gangsters, and only pretend to be real ones, when convenient. Yet, when real things happen, they show their true colours. When it's "I got your back", it turns into, "I had nothing to do with this", especially when caught by themselves. Cowards.

This reminds me of certain Caucasians who are trying to be Black. You know the type that want to play gangster, by having tons of tattoos, and wearing baggy clothing, all while hoping to be surrounded by groups of Blacks. They are a prime example of fake riders, for they are nothing real. Their lifestyle is completely fabricated, which is to manufacture something, especially an industrial product, especially from prepared components. So, they are taking from the originals, and running with it, while not living that true "gangster" lifestyle, nor coming from that environment. Anyone believing that image, is a fool, for that is false living, knowing they can't surviving in the woods of the hoods (Street life). They are quick to put that baseball cap forward, and tell on you when things go sour. This is why Blacks need to not allow them to join in, nor allow them to pretend while fake riding with them. This also reminds me of one known fake gangster rapper who snitched on everyone of the members who were supporting him for the money. They used him, or should I say, a fair trade off, as he got to promote being a "real blood" gang member, while they stood behind him in his music videos, and he knew what he was doing. This character was acting very bad-ass, until all fell down, then he was quick to not take the gangster role on, and quickly put on his true pants, while calling out names, when police busted them for criminal activity. This clown got to go free, while they others are locked up for years to come, and will not see freedom for a very long time. Another set up for destruction. This is why, I do not even hang out, nor acquaint myself with those types of Caucasians who think that they are gangsters. This only annoys me because I know that where they came from, is no where close to the struggles that our people came from, and I'm not saying that we are all Black gangsters, for we are not. I'm saying that, the image that they were hating on for so long, and now acquired, is something they are trying to promote, while I cannot support it, knowing it is not real from the soil. They are not real. They desire to be us, and put themselves in a situation where they had no purpose being in. If you grew up on the greener side of the grass, don't cut that grass for it to appear as it looks like on the other side, for no one on this side of unpleasant grass, wants to stay on this side. We all want better for our lives. So any man that wants to take away from his life, hoping to gain some form of respect from another nation of people, is no man to me, but a confused set of people that have no idea. When they are trying to walk like a gangster, talk like a gangster, and portray a lifestyle that they do not even know the origins about, it is disgusting to witness, and I can't respect it.

Sometimes there will be people who are loud speakers. Those who talk a lot and in most cases are disrespectful towards others. Do not ride with them. For they show off, especially when in large groups, while you know that they are not solid individuals, and are weak. They take advantage of the situation, and join in when convenient. It's easier for them to show off when they're in groups, for others against your group, will resist temptation of trying you all. That one individual is the trouble-maker and is the mouth that speaks much things, while depending on the actions of others to keep them safe.

Ecclesiasticus 08:3

<u>King James Version</u>

3 Strive not with a man that is full of tongue,
   and heap not wood upon his fire.

As you can see in the scripture above, "Strive not with a man that is full of tongue", that is exactly what I said, for that person in going to talk a lot of shit where he may just get you in trouble, somehow, someway. The thing about groups, at times they must walk alone, as individuals, and if you are caught with that mouthy talker, you will end up paying for his loose lips. When you are in affiliation, you have no choice but to take all that comes your way as a whole. When it says, "heap not wood upon his fire", that means, to not be as he is, nor gas him up. For if you boast him up, you are only supporting a fake person, and are shown to be the same. Don't allow a talker to be around you. This is something that I made sure to do, while growing up. No one fake, who runs their mouth, will be able to use my size as protection.

This is why you must always move in respect. Move with people that show the same characteristics as yourself, and if you don't, be sure to correct those along the way, for it will only lead to trouble your way. If you think that it is acceptable, be ready for the retaliation, and responsibilities that come along with it. When you move in respect, which is the best way to me, you get respect in return. When you move in truth, and in reality, you get recognized the same, for real recognize real. Don't ride with fakes, for they will only set you up for destruction.

CHAPTER
THREE

KNOW WHEN TO RIDE

"A true rider
knows when to ride.
A true rider
is not scared to come outside.
A true rider
makes smart moves.
A true rider
wants his team to win
and never lose.
A true rider
tells it like it is.
A true rider
knows when to mind his biz.
A true rider
remains true
cause that's all a true rider
knows what to do.
A true rider
is just like me,
loyal to the death,
filled with truth and honesty.

Knowing when to ride is important. For there will be times where you show your loyalty, and still, choose the better option of not riding. There is nothing wrong with pulling out at times, when you know you are against the cause. Just as I mentioned in the previous chapter, when you move in respect, and is real, respect will come your way regardless, as well as, you will be recognized as a real one. There may be times when your people may just be in the wrong, without accepting it, yet you know that they are in the wrong, and may do something that is not called for. Knowing that there are people who do such things without a cause, but for non other than for "show off" purposes, going below, and beyond to be disrespectful. Such things you should not supported. Your loyalty will not be questioned if you tell that person the truth. Tell them that they are wrong, and you will not support it. For there are people who get this term "ride" the wrong way, where they think they must agree with everything, and be up for all things. No! You can ride while being still. You can easily show the difference, and be the difference, in action, by using your voice to speak truth.

Speak against the wrong, and support the right. We all need someone in our corner who is honest, and real. Being real, is being honest, and upfront, as well as doing the right things that matter in the end. For in most cases, after the doing is done, they may think about what you had informed them of later, and come back to you, while admitting they were wrong. This reminds me of a movie scene within the movie "Boyz n the Hood", where one of the main characters witnessed his friend die before his face, while holding him in his arms, filled with blood, as he screams for help. That same friend, and the brother of the fallen, even a few more within that group, would go out later that night looking for revenge. As the main character was in the back seat, riding along with guns, he decided to back out of the dealing. At that present moment, the rest of them let him out, and didn't care for him, as they carried out that mission that same night. Later finding the individuals responsible, and ending up killing them all. As the next day came, the brother of the fallen, went over to the main character and told him, "it's good you didn't come, as it's haunting me" for killing those others.

This also applies to family. At times someone in your family may just be out of line, and doing something unto another individual, who may not have provoked your sibling. Your sibling may be the aggressor, and needs to be checked, yet the person attacked decides to attack your sibling, and you need to know when to ride. You certainly can step up and support your sibling, however, defuse the situation, instead of adding on to it. You can correct your sibling, while that person who was wronged, should be calmed down and told how it's best to let it go. For no one would want to see their sibling hurt, yet if you are righteous, and know the truth of how it may feel being the one hurt, you must make sure that you sibling understands the consequences, as well as that person who is hurt, to know that they don't need to worry, confirming the hurt that the infliction inflicted was not right. If that individual continues, they of course you must ride with your sibling, for blood comes before a stranger, yet righteousness comes before all.

There was a time where one of my nieces were troubled by her actions towards him. Leaving him in a destination without transportation to get home. Unfortunately he had to end up walking. Though he didn't go home, he came towards my mother's house, and that is a huge problem already. Though young, still stupid. My niece was clearly in the wrong, for they worked things out later, however, we as uncles made sure to show out and allow him to know not to cross any form of line. We had no choice but to stand up for our own, even when wrong, and that is why we did not harm him. Nothing serious happened, for he walked away peacefully. As it could have went in a different direction, it ended with my elder brother and I giving him advice on how to focus on himself, and to not waste time with anyone who treats you unkindly. We also informed him, though they may have caught up in a argument, and it could have been more physical, as my niece did put hands on him. By mentioning the obvious was necessary, and that was, "as it's our blood, no matter what she does to you, we will on see what you do in return physically, and defend our own, especially as she is a female." So, we made sure to defuse the situations while still going back and talking to our niece, correcting her wrong, and why it is important to not put us, nor others in a situation, where we can be in danger, as well as that individual likewise. We told her to always treat people as you would like to be treated. Now, if this was a situation where it was a male sibling friend, who is a male. We would know when to ride, by allowing them to face one another, and put hands up, settling the difference on their own, yet keeping an eye so that it doesn't go to far either way. Same thing applies for when your people may be up against one individual. I believe in a fair fight.

You must decide when to ride, and know when it is worth it, or not. As you do not want to regret anything at all. Yes, anger can lead you to many things, yet, you should go off of instinct, and calculation of the mind. Think things thoroughly through. When you are up against your loyal friends, be sure to not care to be that one who gives sound mind, for without it, you will all fall. Be smart and always keep the codes of ethics, which are important to comply too.

CHAPTER FOUR

RIDE WITH A PURPOSE

"If I'm gonna ride,
I'm gonna ride with a purpose.
Never will I take my life for granted
because it's just not worthless.
I'm trying to show you
how much your worth is.
Loyal to the soil
no matter how deep this earth is.
Nothing, doesn't mean something.
And just as long as my heart keep thumping
I'm with you to the end,
doing something for nothing,
for you can't put a price on love.
For life without purpose, is worthless"

I'm a man that likes doing things with a purpose, with a plan, and doing so, with meaning behind all that I do. I dislike doing things that makes no sense. If I'm not benefiting from that which I am doing, then it is pointless. When you ride with a purpose, you must know what benefits will be there to you, or the person that you are riding with. It can be quality time spent. It can be to accomplish a goal together. It can be to prove a point. It can be many things, unmentioned. All of which mean something. It's like going to work. You work for the payment, and if you own the company, you are working for quality, and promoting your product as best as possible. You want the best outcome either way. For if you want that payment, your purpose for working hard is to secure that income in which can support you further along the way. Pushing that product in a good manner, gives you customers that will keep coming back for service.

If you ever been in a situation where you are doing something that makes no sense, that is losing time, effort, and purpose. It will not help you at any time.

I look at situations where people are so lame. Certain individuals who are simple minded, and take away from others lives, by doing pranks, being ass-holes, and treating others unfairly, through harassment. They are evil people that have too much time on their hands, yet without a purpose to pursue.

Psalm 69:4
<u>King James Version</u>

4 They that hate me without a cause are more than the hairs of mine head: they that would destroy me, being mine enemies wrongfully, are mighty: then I restored that which I took not away.

Many people out there will attack you thinking that you are a push over, and easy to destroy. They ride without a purpose, but need to understand, creating any form of beef is dangerous, and consequences will happen. Imagine tormenting someone without a purpose, and taking away from that persons life? I tell you, you better have a purpose, for the person that is being attacked is not going to be happy. My whole thing is, why go and do things unto others who do not deserve it, nor have time for your stupidity, and ignorance? We all have life to life, and because you have more time on your hand, doesn't give you the opportunity to disrespect anyone, nor take away from their responsibilities. Being a thorn in someones behind, only makes that person you are harassing, having no choice but to deal with the thorn. That thorn is time. That time is now taking away from time for other responsibilities. No one deserve to deal with that. For everything there should be a purpose, and with that purpose, have a responsible, mature way to handle those situations. For the level and measure of ignorance that you do unto another, that person can now come back at you however which way they desire, knowing you are tampering with their lives.

Your purpose in riding should always be beneficial and always remember to make it count. Profit in all areas is important. This doesn't only mean financially. Gain spiritually, mentally, and as a person with the qualities necessary to make one better.

CHAPTER FIVE

RIDING? DON'T NEED TO ASK

"When you're riding,
you don't need to ask.
Load up,
everyone's on deck
and we ready to blast.
We move quick,
and defeat the enemy fast.
Real recognize real,
and that's how we last.
Respecting the ways of old,
times past.
Time, keeps ticking
and keeps ticking fast.
No need to worry,
I will never change nor put on a mask.
I remain the same,
as long as you do too.
Be there for me,
and I'll be there for you.
That way,
we will always make just due,
for this is the things that real love
makes one do."

There are times when someone wants you to ride with them, but are afraid to ask. Maybe not wanting to involve you. If you are a real friend, you volunteer to ride without question. For no one should ask you to do anything that you should know your role in doing. If you're a rider, there is no need to ask, just go. It's like when you are in a situation, as simple as needing a help with your car. Your friends, or family, should be the front liners to arrive, and help assist you out of that trouble. Your situations, should be there situations, and vice-versa. That is loyalty, and proves that love is one. If you have people as so in your connection, that support factor is major, and will certainly benefit you along your journey. For when one hurts, the rest should help heal. When one falls, the others should aim that one up. It's all about the support system that needs to be established, in order for that foundation to operate smoothly.

There is nothing like a true friend, even within the family, who is there for you when all is gone. They are willing to put you up, until you get back on your feet. No questions asked. We all know how hard life is, and how important it is for support to always be there from your own. Your own is important, for without that stability, it show loose ends, and that at times is a good thing, however, not so when it comes down to your family, and so called "friends'. For family, they will always be family, but friends, always have the opportunity to walk out of your life, just as much as you can remove them from your life the same. Try your best to always sift through the real from the fake, and when you do come across fake ones, be sure to separate yourselves from them. If it comes to family, I know how difficult this may be, due to honouring your mother, and father's name. Yet, it is always best to be the example, and not the example. Just as I wrote in my other book by the same title, "Be the Example, NOT the Example".

When you are the example, you are showing that you do not need to be like the rest of them, but be you, by showing that you are different, and even if that means doing the things that they do not do. It's like tit-for-tat, which is doing something only if you do it first, or that is the only time he/she is willing to do it in return. If you miss your turn, they take record. That is foolish, and childish. It is best to always be the example, and not the example. If you are the example, which is what you can also use as a positive, knowing the bad example set forth, is what not to do. An example of that is, someone who is cooking a meal, and that person doesn't offer you a plate, for what ever reasons. Yet you were all there, and hungry. Now, when the tables are turned and you are cooking your meal, while everyone is hungry, you share. That is a prime example of being the example, and not the example. The good example, is to give, when you know all is hungry, and without. The bad example, is to be greedy, and only care for yourself, while all else desires a plate. You will only be looked upon as the terrible individual that is selfish. Sometimes this may just happen in your household, hopefully not though, as this is just an example. Yet there are situations similar to this, which can certainly occur.

We all need to be that same good example and help thy brother/sister in times of trouble without having to be asked. We all fall into ditches at certain points in our lives, and for some, we tend to tell those who we are surrounded by, just to share the bad news. Those same ones hearing the bad news, know you came to them to tell them the story, just to know you can lean on their shoulders, even for verbal support. It's up to those same shoulders to then realize that they can make the best out of the situation for you if they have the means to do so. Many times in my life, this has happened, and I'm thankful to have certain family members that reached out and helped me along the way, mainly my mother, who is just as myself, who would give if we got it to give, or help in any way possible.

Be careful of victims who only want to take and not give. No one owes nobody anything. For there will be people who tend to try and act as if they deserve something from you, just because. They will play victim as they desire to want, and continue to take without having efforts of helping self. They will use you, and then curse you out when your back is turned, or your hand is no longer available, to feed them. Those who behave in such manner, should not be apart of your circle, for they will only stir up strife, and have you question their purpose surround you. Not too much fit this category, however, the worst case, is when all sees that you are in need of assistance, however which way, and hold their silence, while many may even have the means, yet do nothing to support your efforts. That is cold. However, you can turn it around for the positive, if you would like, as you can use that opportunity to grow on your own, and gain what you needed through experience, instead of someone handing you that information, that payout, that support. Yet, it is good to have those surrounding you who would at least offer, which would make it more of a comforting settings. For again, I've been in situations, where many times, family would offer, and I would refuse the help, as I knew certain things I must be able to do on my own. Which brings me to the next chapter, "Ride alone, handle your business".

CHAPTER
SIX

RIDE ALONE
(HANDLE YOUR BUSINESS)

"When you ride alone,
it's something you can handle.
Sort of like lighting match to a candle.
Once you light the match,
that spark starts the flame.
It lights up the room,
and that's when you realize
not everyone is riding the same.
At no time do we point the finger and blame
nor do we ever point the trigger and take aim.
We men,
and we do what men do.
Stand on your feet,
and remain on your two.
In all things that you do,
always remain true.
Never sellout
because you never know
who in this world
could be watching you.
Handle your business,
stand firm like a tree.
This is your journey
be where you got to be."

When riding, sometimes you should know that it is best to ride alone. Certain situations, need a resolution from yourself. Certain matters that come up, are required to be taken on by self, and no other. Even when others volunteer, and want to ride with you, you decline the offer, and ride alone. Not all wars are meant to be fought with an army. Certain things are personal. Sometimes the journey is meant to be for yourself, to lose, to gain, to slip, to rise, and to experience, and learn along the way. It's also to prove unto yourself and unto others, that you are capable of handling your own business as a man. Just as I mentioned a few chapters back about that clown that had a so called "beef" with me, and could not even face me, yet recruited others to join in, and fight his battle for him. That is a prime example of not being able to prove himself, and that is why I cannot accept him as a man, but as a coward. For he is not a boss, but a punk.

There will be times when handling your business alone, will prove to yourself that you are no punk, especially when you are going up against punks. I will use that same situation with the clown that I was referring to before, who was such a tough guy towards his wife, while being a coward towards me. As I have people that could easily defend me, I chose to not rely upon them. I have a Mighty YAH (God), who is there for me always. Yet, these cowards that this loser needed to support him, while hiding away, were no match for me, that I should be afraid of, and depend upon others. They were so weak and cowardly as mentioned before that they moved even weaker than that loser of a clown. This would only make me come off weak if I were to seek help, and assistance from others. So, in my case, this was personal, and not worth the aid from loyal loved ones. For when you see the people, you would laugh, and I would feel embarrassed. The Most High made me strong, and most things, I handle on my own, just because I am independent, and move accordingly with respect. The only ones who disrespect me, hide themselves, and don't ever face me while doing so.

There are times when you do not want to get others involved, nor put them in danger, and that is important to avoid. There is a lot of people being persecuted, and found guilty by affiliation. This is a dangerous thing, for certain people that can assist you, even by giving you direction, can end up being locked up, if a serious matter shall happen, knowing they assisted you. So, with that said, avoid situations as much as possible, by limiting those involved in serious matters. Love is love, and love will always support you, however, sometimes love is more important to protect, and by protecting love, you are saving lives, and doing more for love, than love is doing for you.

CHAPTER
SEVEN

RIDE OUT
(SOMETHING ABOUT LOYALTY)

"There's something about loyalty,
that makes me feel good.
Honour and respect.
Care with the love.
I owe everything I got
to the Most High above.
HE made me see life
for what it really is.
Went through long suffering
even growing up as a kid.
The trials and tribulations,
made this journey all worth it.
This life, I'm so blessed
that no man can curse it.
My destination is quite clear
knowing I'm right there.
The end of the tunnel.
Got to make my way through.
Salvation,
is the promise
that we all hold onto.
YAH
I seek your face,
and I'm thankful that I found you.
No other god can ever take your place"

RIDE OUT!

This may sound contradicting to some, as you may have read from the previous chapter, how you should ride alone at times, and for this chapter, for people to go all out in riding. Well, just know that you make the difference, and as you look out for your loved ones, you are setting a huge foundation of loyalty, and a message of security, that you are always going to ride out with them. There is something about loyalty that shows love more than measurable. When that rider is in your life, sort of like a wife to a husband, when he loses his job, and she is still there, while not thinking about leaving him due to financial matters. There is something about a friend who has your back, even when you are not there to defend you. A loved one, within your family that smiles, and thinks about you, without a cause, just because you are special unto them.

Loyalty is everything. Honour, is a part of it, and those who have it in them, keep promises, and never falter. When it's time to ride out, and all goes down, those names that have been there, never change. Those who are soldiers and riders, will be remembered, and kept in the memory of those who witnessed there loyal behaviour unto the cause, and that will not leave them.

Proverbs 18:24
<u>King James Version</u>

24 A man that hath friends must shew himself friendly: and there is a friend that sticketh closer than a brother.

We must know that through all the loyalty that we have for man in this world, we must have deeper loyalty to the Creator, who is the Most High YAH (God), LORD of lords, and KING of kings. The Alpha and the Omega, the beginning and the ending. That is where my loyalty is most, and is well before man, for to me the Most High is my LORD. I must serve my YAH (God) before man. For the likeness of my Heavenly Father, is more better than the respect of persons. Since my mother had taught me about the Bible, as a teenager, I took advantage of reading it, and finding the truth. Ever since then, my adult life has been serving HIM. I've been a faithful rider nonetheless. Though at times I may have had little faith, I still kept HIM as my YAH (God). I have been making pictures with scripture verses, hoping to help other read the Bible, and continue to remain there. All it takes is a nudge in the right direction of hope. Here is a few of the work that I have done while doing graphic design. I usually gave them away for free, more than selling them.

My advertising ad

SIZE	W/OUT PICTURE FRAME	W/ PICTURE FRAME
8 X 10	$5.00	$10.00
11 X 14	$10.00	$18.00
16 x 20	$15.00	$20.00

* MORE SIZES AVAILABLE UPON REQUEST
CONTACT EMAIL WITH YOUR NAME, PHONE NUMBER, AND PICTURE REQUEST ALONG WITH SIZE OF PICTURE

PEACE
DEPART FROM EVIL, AND DO GOOD;
SEEK PEACE, AND PURSUE IT.
- PSALM 34:14 (KJV) -

What therefore God hath joined
together, let not man put asunder.
Mark 10:9
(King James Version)

For with GOD nothing shall be impossible.
Luke 1:37
King James Version

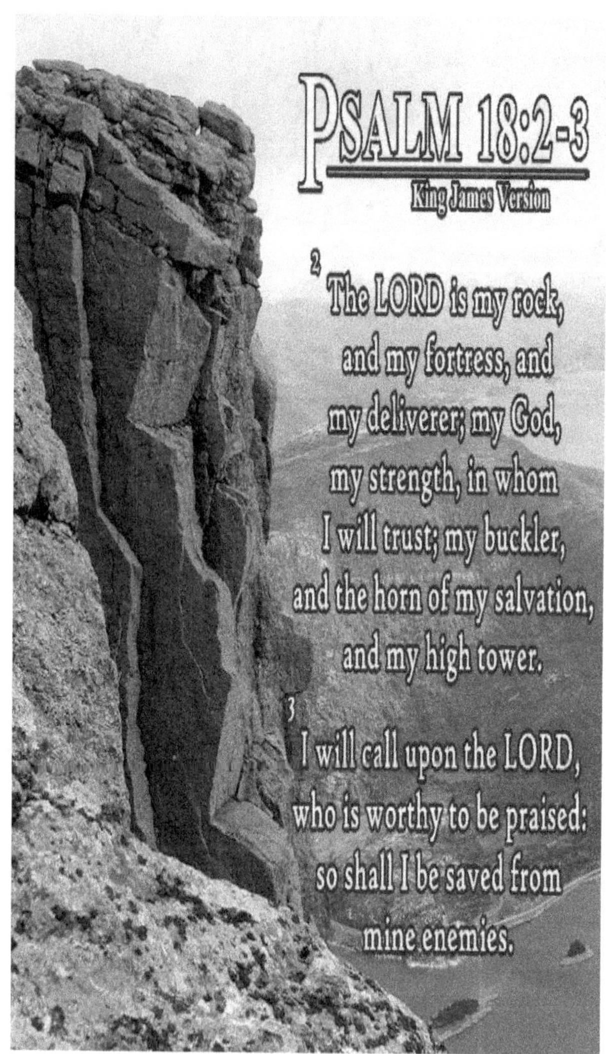
PSALM 18:2-3
King James Version

2 The LORD is my rock,
and my fortress, and
my deliverer; my God,
my strength, in whom
I will trust; my buckler,
and the horn of my salvation,
and my high tower.

3 I will call upon the LORD,
who is worthy to be praised:
so shall I be saved from
mine enemies.

As you can see, I'm writing, and have many books that are inspired by the gospel, and have been motivating people ever since, as well as making sure to share this wisdom that I have obtained through my own long-suffering, trials, and tribulations. Sharing the experiences that I have been through, hoping that you, the reader can relate.

We must all know when to respect one another choices, and those choices, may not include you, making it not personal at all, but a deeper understanding of self, and connection with the Father. We are here on a mission, and we must stick to our mission, which is more important than anything going on in our personal lives. Just like Jonah, who went astray from his mission, got put right back on track, and was needed to ride out, for he had to do for HIS Father, more than what he wanted to do for self. For we must obey the calling when being called. And this call is most important, more than any family member, nor friend who may be in distress. For this calling, is going to assist many lives more than one. How much are you willing to do for loyalty? How much time are you willing to put into the work of the LORD? Same question can apply in reverse to the haters, how much time are you going to take robbing YAH (God) children from doing HIS work? For we must all know that time is nothing to play around with, yet so many people have time to alter the courses of other people, who are in this truth, spreading the gospel, such as myself.

Personally, the most loyal person to me, is my YAH (God). For HE has been there for me since I've been in the womb of my mother, even before that. And I never knew HIM until my teenage years. How could that be? Well, that is the love that a Father has for HIS son. We as Israelites are the children of the Most High, and HE has been loyal to us since before our time, for our Israelite forefathers has been under HIS protection ever since.

2 Esdras 1
<u>King James Version</u>

1 The second book of the prophet Esdras, the son of Saraias, the son of Azarias, the son of Helchias, the son of Sadamias, the son of Sadoc, the son of Achitob,

2 The son of Achias, the son of Phinees, the son of Heli, the son of Amarias, the son of Aziei, the son of Marimoth, the son of Arna, the son of Ozias, the son of Borith, the son of Abisei, the son of Phinees, the son of Eleazar,

3 The son of Aaron, of the tribe of Levi; which was captive in the land of the Medes, in the reign of Artexerxes king of the Persians.

4 And the word of the Lord came unto me, saying,

5 Go thy way, and shew my people their sinful deeds, and their children their wickedness which they have done against me; that they

may tell their children's children:

6 Because the sins of their fathers are increased in them: for they have forgotten me, and have offered unto strange gods.

7 Am not I even he that brought them out of the land of Egypt, from the house of bondage? but they have provoked me unto wrath, and despised my counsels.

8 Pull thou off then the hair of thy head, and cast all evil upon them, for they have not been obedient unto my law, but it is a rebellious people.

9 How long shall I forbear them, into whom I have done so much good?

10 Many kings have I destroyed for their sakes; Pharaoh with his servants and all his power have I smitten down.

11 All the nations have I destroyed before them, and in the east I have scattered the people of two provinces, even of Tyrus and Sidon, and have slain all their enemies.

12 Speak thou therefore unto them, saying,
Thus saith the Lord,

13 I led you through the sea and in the
beginning gave you a large and safe passage; I
gave you Moses for a leader, and Aaron for a
priest.

14 I gave you light in a pillar of fire, and great
wonders have I done among you; yet have ye
forgotten me, saith the Lord.

15 Thus saith the Almighty Lord, The quails
were as a token to you; I gave you tents for
your safeguard: nevertheless ye murmured
there,

16 And triumphed not in my name for the
destruction of your enemies, but ever to this
day do ye yet murmur.

17 Where are the benefits that I have done for
you? when ye were hungry and thirsty in the
wilderness, did ye not cry unto me,

18 Saying, Why hast thou brought us into this

wilderness to kill us? it had been better for us to have served the Egyptians, than to die in this wilderness.

19 Then had I pity upon your mournings, and gave you manna to eat; so ye did eat angels' bread.

20 When ye were thirsty, did I not cleave the rock, and waters flowed out to your fill? for the heat I covered you with the leaves of the trees.

21 I divided among you a fruitful land, I cast out the Canaanites, the Pherezites, and the Philistines, before you: what shall I yet do more for you? saith the Lord.

22 Thus saith the Almighty Lord, When ye were in the wilderness, in the river of the Amorites, being athirst, and blaspheming my name,

23 I gave you not fire for your blasphemies, but cast a tree in the water, and made the river sweet.

24 What shall I do unto thee, O Jacob? thou,

Juda, wouldest not obey me: I will turn me to other nations, and unto those will I give my name, that they may keep my statutes.

25 Seeing ye have forsaken me, I will forsake you also; when ye desire me to be gracious unto you, I shall have no mercy upon you.

26 Whensoever ye shall call upon me, I will not hear you: for ye have defiled your hands with blood, and your feet are swift to commit manslaughter.

27 Ye have not as it were forsaken me, but your own selves, saith the Lord.

28 Thus saith the Almighty Lord, Have I not prayed you as a father his sons, as a mother her daughters, and a nurse her young babes,

29 That yc would be my people, and I should be your God; that ye would be my children, and I should be your father?

30 I gathered you together, as a hen gathereth her chickens under her wings: but now, what shall I do unto you? I will cast you out from

my face.

31 When ye offer unto me, I will turn my face from you: for your solemn feastdays, your new moons, and your circumcisions, have I forsaken.

32 I sent unto you my servants the prophets, whom ye have taken and slain, and torn their bodies in pieces, whose blood I will require of your hands, saith the Lord.

33 Thus saith the Almighty Lord, Your house is desolate, I will cast you out as the wind doth stubble.

34 And your children shall not be fruitful; for they have despised my commandment, and done the thing that is an evil before me.

35 Your houses will I give to a people that shall come; which not having heard of me yet shall believe me; to whom I have shewed no signs, yet they shall do that I have commanded them.

36 They have seen no prophets, yet they shall call their sins to remembrance, and

acknowledge them.

37 I take to witness the grace of the people to come, whose little ones rejoice in gladness: and though they have not seen me with bodily eyes, yet in spirit they believe the thing that I say.

38 And now, brother, behold what glory; and see the people that come from the east:

39 Unto whom I will give for leaders, Abraham, Isaac, and Jacob, Oseas, Amos, and Micheas, Joel, Abdias, and Jonas,

40 Nahum, and Abacuc, Sophonias, Aggeus, Zachary, and Malachy, which is called also an angel of the Lord.

2 Esdras 2:1-17
King James Version

1 Thus saith the Lord, I brought this people out of bondage, and I gave them my commandments by menservants the prophets; whom they would not hear, but despised my counsels.

2 The mother that bare them saith unto them,
Go your way, ye children; for I am a widow
and forsaken.

3 I brought you up with gladness; but with
sorrow and heaviness have I lost you: for ye
have sinned before the Lord your God, and
done that thing that is evil before him.

4 But what shall I now do unto you? I am a
widow and forsaken: go your way, O my
children, and ask mercy of the Lord.

5 As for me, O father, I call upon thee for a
witness over the mother of these children,
which would not keep my covenant,

6 That thou bring them to confusion, and their
mother to a spoil, that there may be no
offspring of them.

7 Let them be scattered abroad among the
heathen, let their names be put out of the earth:
for they have despised my covenant.

8 Woe be unto thee, Assur, thou that hidest the

unrighteous in thee! O thou wicked people, remember what I did unto Sodom and Gomorrha;

9 Whose land lieth in clods of pitch and heaps of ashes: even so also will I do unto them that hear me not, saith the Almighty Lord.

10 Thus saith the Lord unto Esdras, Tell my people that I will give them the kingdom of Jerusalem, which I would have given unto Israel.

11 Their glory also will I take unto me, and give these the everlasting tabernacles, which I had prepared for them.

12 They shall have the tree of life for an ointment of sweet savour; they shall neither labour, nor be weary.

13 Go, and ye shall receive: pray for few days unto you, that they may be shortened: the kingdom is already prepared for you: watch.

14 Take heaven and earth to witness; for I have broken the evil in pieces, and created the good:

for I live, saith the Lord.

15 Mother, embrace thy children, and bring them up with gladness, make their feet as fast as a pillar: for I have chosen thee, saith the Lord.

16 And those that be dead will I raise up again from their places, and bring them out of the graves: for I have known my name in Israel.

17 Fear not, thou mother of the children: for I have chosen thee, saith the Lord.

When it's time to ride out, I'm riding with the LORD, and the only begotten son of the Father, who is Christ. For when the war starts, which has already been formed and is actually begun, I'm riding out with the right team. As I spread the message of truth, even through these books of mine. The true gospel will be told, and those who learn, and agree, will join the battle, while being on the right side as well. Evil is in this world, and we all know their tactics, through their shown iniquity, and deceiving ways. We must know that we are strong for a reason, and the struggle of longsuffering was important for us to endure, so that we can survive until the end. We are stronger than the enemy, for our YAH (God), has already foretold the story of the saints. For a saint is just a sinner who fell down, and got back up. We are all going to repent, and turn from evil, while turning to the righteousness, through repentance, that will bring us closer to the Most High, just as much as we will draw HIM nigh unto us.

James 4:8
King James Version

8 Draw nigh to God, and he will draw nigh to you. Cleanse your hands, ye sinners; and purify your hearts, ye double minded.

RIDE OUT!

LIST OF SOURCES

- The Holy Bible (King James Version)
- The Apocrypha (King James Version)

YOU CAN'T WIN WITH JEALOUSY
WRITTEN BY:
DEVRET CLARKE

WHAT
HAPPENED
TO THE
MANLY
MAN
?
DEVRET CLARKE

DEVRET CLARKE
No Sympathy For The Wicked

DEVRET CLARKE
EXPOSING
THE WAYS OF THE
WICKED

THE NARROW PATH
WRITTEN BY:
DEVRET CLARKE

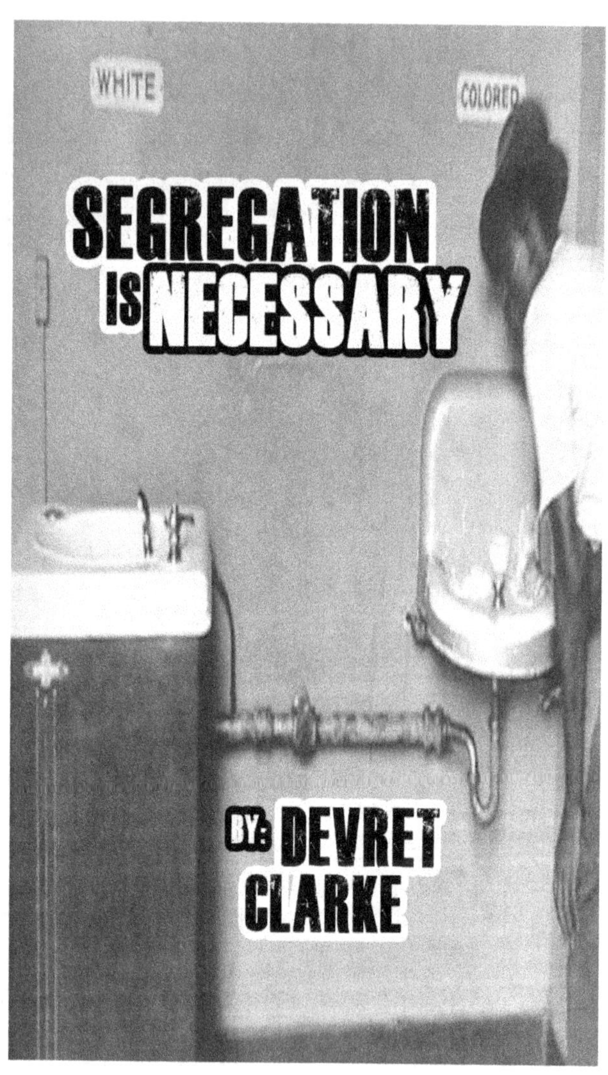
WHITE
COLORED
SEGREGATION IS NECESSARY
BY: DEVRET CLARKE

WHITE
COLORED
SEGREGATION
IS NECESSARY
2
EXPOSING
THE
ENEMY
BY: DEVRET
CLARKE

Still Sleeping?
WAKE UP!
Dedicated to the 12 TRIBES of ISRAEL
WRITTEN BY:
DEVRET CLARKE

Still Sleeping?
WAKE UP!
PART 2
WRITTEN BY:
DEVRET CLARKE
DEDICATED TO THE 12 TRIBES OF ISRAEL

We All Go Through It,
The Journey Called
"LIFE"
WRITTEN BY:
DEVRET CLARKE

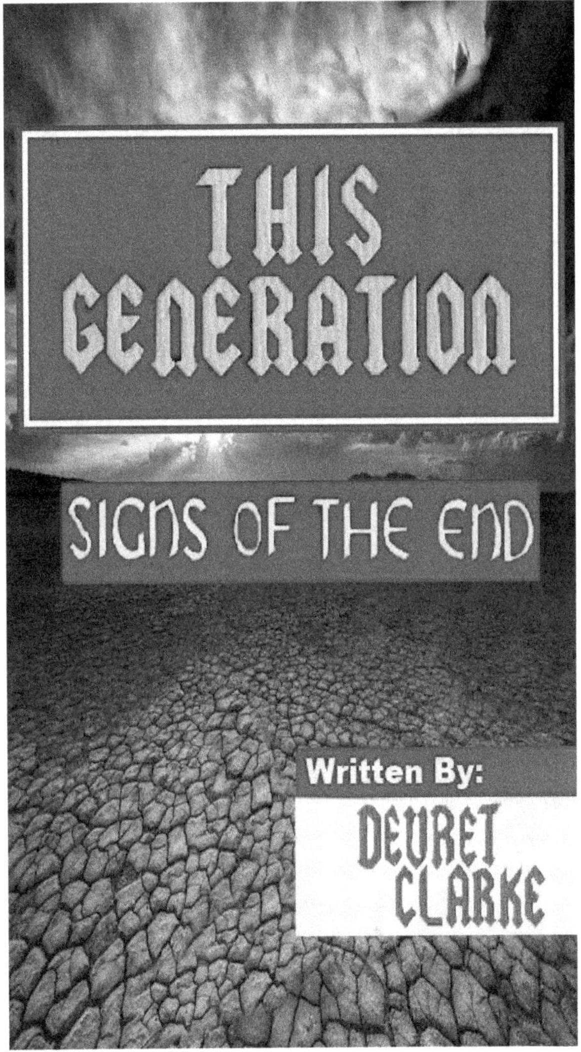
THIS
GENERATION
SIGNS OF THE END
Written By:
DEVRET CLARKE

DEVRET
CLARKE

REAL TALK
JUST SPEAKING MY MIND

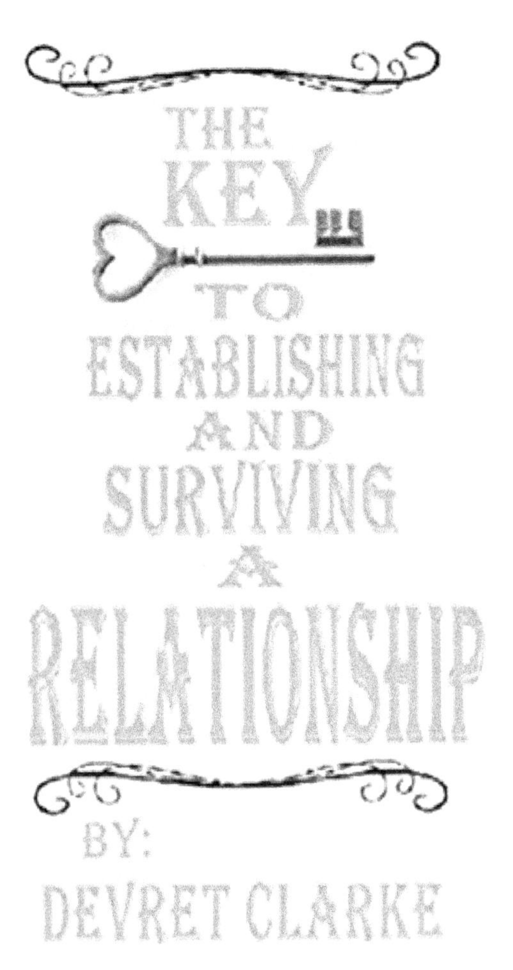
THE
KEY
TO
ESTABLISHING
AND
SURVIVING
A
RELATIONSHIP
BY:
DEVRET CLARKE

by: DEVRET CLARKE
LOVE
IS NOT LOVE,
UNTIL LOVE
LOVES YOU...

BY: DEVRET
CLARKE
FOR THE
HATERS

DEVRET CLARKE
USED

DEVRET
CLARKE
BE
THE
EXAMPLE
NOT
THE
EXAMPLE

Devret Clarke
MIRRORS
Do you believe yourself?

THE
RIGHTEOUS
WALK
What Happened to
Morals and Values ?
DEVRET
CLARKE

DEVRET CLARKE
THE INTERNET ERROR
THE SURVIVAL OF HUMANITY

DEVRET CLARKE
THROUGH THE STORM
THE BENEFITS OF
LONGSUFFERING

THE WAR OF WORDS
Written By:
Devret Clarke

THE
TEMPORARY
VOICES INSIDE
MY HEAD
Devret Clarke
Facing:
Unwanted Telepathy, witchcraft, sorcery, & "Gang-stalking"

KNOW WHEN TO RIDE
DEVRET CLARKE

Book Author,
DEVRET CLARKE
Website - DevretClarke.ca
WAKE UP!
WAKE UP! 2

Like what you read?
Support the author. All blessings are appreciated.

https://www.paypal.com/donate?
hosted_button_id=TMM43TPRV2VTN